From **BROKEN** to ***Becoming*:**

Running and Evolving into Grace

Melissa Richey-Bridges

The testimonies shared in this book reflect the personal experiences and perspectives of the contributors. Names, identifying details, and circumstances may have been changed to protect privacy. The views expressed are those of the individual contributors and do not necessarily reflect those of the publisher.

This book is intended for inspirational and informational purposes only and is not a substitute for professional, medical, legal, or therapeutic advice.

All contributors have granted permission for their stories to be included in this work.

Table of Contents

Introduction:

On March 30, 2025, I turned 45. To celebrate, I took a solo trip that took me to the breathtaking shores of Phuket, Thailand, the vibrant city of Kuala Lumpur, Malaysia, and the tranquil beauty of Bali, Indonesia. It was more than a vacation. It was a journey of self-discovery, healing, and reconnecting with God.

While in Bali, I did a photoshoot in a stunning gold dress. In one moment, the photographer captured me running, followed by a slow-motion twirl. The freedom I felt in that moment was unlike any other, and it was in that fleeting, yet powerful space that I wrote something for my social media. I want to share that with you:

When you get tired of running from the same thing that's causing you pain…

Run into the arms of the One who won't let you break, God.

He won't just catch you, He'll carry you.

Start your healing, from the inside out.

Let Him restore what life tried to steal.

Let Him silence the lies you've believed about yourself.

Let Him remind you that you were never too broken to be made whole.

This is your moment:
To be free

To be blessed
To be authentically you
To rise up from the ashes
To be grateful even in the growing

Stop running from pain. Start running toward purpose.

As I sat in the Istanbul airport on a layover, I revisited that caption, and something inside me stirred. In that quiet moment, I made a decision, I would write this book.

I hope this book inspires you to stop running from your pain and start running toward your purpose. May it encourage you to trust in God's ability to carry you when you feel like you can't go any further, and remind you that healing is possible, even in the most broken places. You are not too far gone to be made whole. No matter where you are in life, no matter the pain you've endured, this is your moment to evolve into the person you were always meant to be.

You, too, can rise from the ashes. You can be free, be blessed, and embrace the life you were created to live. This book is not just my story, it's yours too. Let's run together, toward grace, toward healing, and toward purpose.

Dedication

This book is dedicated to everyone who has ever faced adversity, whether it was a broken heart, a shattered dream, or a moment that left you questioning everything.

To those who have fought to heal and rebuild, who have stumbled, yet kept going, and who have learned that even in the darkest moments, there is hope.

To the ones who may feel forgotten, lost, or overlooked, know that your story is far from over. You are not defined by your struggles but by your strength to keep moving forward, one step at a time.

And most of all, this book is dedicated to God who carried me through it all, the One who never let me break, but instead, led me into grace. May you, too, find healing and purpose in His embrace.

Chapter 1:
The Pain That Pursues Us: *Recognizing the Wounds and Patterns We Keep Running From*

Have you ever wondered why certain pains seem to follow you, no matter how far you run? Why do we hide from our emotions, and why does it feel like pain finds us no matter where we go? These questions are more than just fleeting thoughts, they are invitations to delve deeper into understanding ourselves.

The Unseen Baggage

We all carry invisible scars; experiences and traumas that, though not seen, profoundly affect our daily lives. These wounds can manifest in various ways:

• Emotional Triggers: Certain situations or words can unexpectedly stir up intense emotions, revealing unresolved issues.

• Behavioral Patterns: Repeated actions, like pushing people away or avoiding commitments, often stem from past hurts.

• Physical Symptoms: Stress and unresolved emotions can manifest as headaches, fatigue, or other physical ailments.

The Temptation to Hide

In an attempt to shield ourselves from further pain, we might resort to hiding:

• Building Walls: Creating emotional barriers to prevent others from getting too close.

• Denial: Pretending issues don't exist, hoping they'll resolve on their own.

• Overcompensation: Being overly busy or involved in distractions to avoid facing our true feelings.

However, hiding doesn't heal. Instead, it prolongs the pain and keeps us tethered to our past.

Facing the Pain

Acknowledging our wounds is the first step toward healing:

• Self-Reflection: Taking time to introspect and identify recurring emotional responses or behaviors.
• Seeking Support: Engaging with trusted friends, family, or professionals who can offer perspective and guidance.
• Embracing Vulnerability: Allowing ourselves to feel and express emotions without judgment.

Reflection:

Think about a recurring pain or challenge in your life. How have you responded to it in the past? Have you noticed any patterns in your reactions? Recognizing these patterns is the first step toward breaking free from them.

Chapter 2:
The Exhaustion of Escape: *What It Costs to Keep Avoiding What Hurts*

Avoiding pain is a natural instinct; we all seek comfort and steer clear of discomfort. However, when avoidance becomes our primary coping mechanism, it exacts a significant toll on our well-being.

The Illusion of Short-Term Relief

In the short term, sidestepping painful emotions or situations may seem beneficial. This avoidance provides immediate relief, allowing us to bypass discomfort temporarily. However, this relief is often fleeting, and the underlying issues persist, sometimes intensifying over time.

The Accumulating Costs of Avoidance

While avoidance might offer temporary respite, the long-term costs are substantial:

- Physical Health Decline: Chronic avoidance can lead to increased stress, manifesting as fatigue, headaches, or more severe health issues.
- Emotional Exhaustion: Suppressing emotions requires significant energy, leading to feelings of burnout, irritability, or emotional numbness.
- Stunted Personal Growth: By not confronting challenges, we miss opportunities for personal development, remaining stagnant in our emotional and psychological journeys.

The Paradox of Avoidance

Attempting to suppress or avoid emotions can be counterproductive. The more we try to ignore or suppress our feelings, the more they can resurface, often more intensely. This paradox means that avoidance doesn't eliminate pain but can amplify it in the long run.

Embracing the Path to Healing

Recognizing the costs of avoidance is the first step toward healing. Embracing our emotions, even the painful ones, allows us to process and move beyond them. This approach leads to:

- Improved Mental Health: Facing our feelings can reduce anxiety, depression, and other mental health challenges.
- Enhanced Relationships: Openly addressing emotions fosters deeper connections and mutual understanding.
- Personal Empowerment: Confronting difficulties builds resilience, confidence, and a sense of ownership over our lives.

Reflection:

Consider areas in your life where you might be avoiding discomfort. How has this avoidance impacted you physically, emotionally, and relationally? Acknowledging these patterns is crucial for initiating change.

Chapter 3:
The Encounter:
Meeting God in Our Lowest Moment

In our darkest hours, when hope seems distant and joy is but a memory, an unexpected presence can emerge, transforming despair into light. This chapter delves into the profound experience of encountering God during our most challenging times, drawing from personal narratives and spiritual insights.

A Personal Descent into Darkness

There was a time when the weight of the world seemed unbearable. Happiness was a foreign concept, and the future appeared shrouded in uncertainty. In this abyss, I found myself questioning not just my circumstances but also my faith. It was a period where every day felt like a battle, and the prospect of victory seemed elusive.

The Divine Intervention

Just as the night is darkest before the dawn, my lowest point became the backdrop for a transformative encounter. In the midst of my anguish, I felt an undeniable presence, a warmth that pierced the coldness of my despair. It was as if God reached into my turmoil, offering solace without words. This experience wasn't marked by visions or audible voices but by an overwhelming sense of peace and assurance that I was not alone.

Scriptural Reflections on Divine Presence

The Bible offers numerous accounts of individuals finding God in their moments of deepest despair:

• Psalm 34:18: "The Lord is close to the brokenhearted and saves those who are crushed in spirit."

• Isaiah 41:10: "So do not fear, for I am with you; do not be dismayed, for I am your God."

• 2 Corinthians 1:3-4: "Praise be to the God and Father of our Lord Jesus Christ, the Father of compassion and the God of all comfort, who comforts us in all our troubles."

Testimonies of Transformation

Many have walked the path from darkness to light, finding God in the very moments they thought they were alone. Healing does not happen in silence, it happens in the stories we dare to tell, and the truth we finally choose to release. God placed it on my heart to reach out to seven women, each carrying her own journey, her own breaking point, and her own breakthrough. Their testimonies are raw, honest, and powerful, and they reveal what happens when grace steps into the room and refuses to let go.

These are not just stories of survival, they are stories of surrender, resilience, and transformation. These women opened their hearts so another woman could find strength, hope, and clarity in her own valley. My prayer is that as you read their journeys, you see reflections of your own, and that something within you begins to heal, rise, and evolve.

My Testimony: Delivered Through the Whirlwind

In 2018, I made the painful but necessary decision to get a divorce. What followed was nothing short of a whirlwind, an unraveling of everything I thought my life would be. I didn't realize it at the time, but God was preparing to take me on a journey that would completely reshape me spiritually, mentally, emotionally, and physically.

I had spent years trying to live up to someone else's definition of a "great wife," slowly losing the very essence of who God created me to be. My self-esteem was nearly nonexistent. I was drained. I wasn't just unhappy, I was depleted. My health in every aspect was failing, and I felt like I was living a life that didn't even belong to me. I wanted out. I needed to breathe. I needed to live, not just exist.

It wasn't until after the divorce process began that I realized God was calling me to be delivered from something much deeper than a broken relationship. I was being delivered from codependency, a soul-binding pattern where I constantly poured into others while abandoning myself. I had unknowingly taken on the role of "the giver," sacrificing my own needs, my voice, and my worth in hopes of keeping the peace, feeling loved, or simply being enough.

In those quiet, painful days, I asked God over and over again, "How did I get here?" I cried often. I felt unmotivated. Alone. But one day, in the middle of my brokenness, I found myself lying on the floor, crying out to God from a place I didn't even know existed within me.

And that's when everything changed. God answered. "The Lord is near to the brokenhearted and saves the crushed in spirit." Psalm 34:18

That moment, raw and unfiltered, was the beginning of something sacred. It was the birth of my prayer life. I didn't have eloquent words or perfect faith. I just had my pain and His presence. And He met me there. In that moment, I realized that nothing is wasted with God.

He took the ashes of my past and began crafting something beautiful. My pain became my prayer. My loss became the foundation of my intimacy with Him. I learned that He doesn't require perfection, He desires surrender. "And we know that in all things God works for the good of those who love Him, who have been called according to His purpose." Romans 8:28

Even now, there are moments when I don't understand what He's doing. There are days when I can't clearly hear Him. But I trust Him because He knew me before I was formed in my mother's womb (Jeremiah 1:5). He wrote my story before I even knew I had a voice in it.

And for that alone, I rejoice and am glad. This journey hasn't been easy, but it has been divine. God has shown me who I truly am in Him: worthy, whole, and deeply loved. Not because of what I can give, but because I belong to Him.

-Aleacha Philson, mother, daughter, friend, Colonel, United States Air Force

My testimony: Survival Mode

At the happiest point in my life, I became a widow. Nine short months after giving birth to our beautiful daughter, I was faced with a painful truth, I would have to raise her alone. She would be another fatherless child. In that moment, I entered survival mode. As a mother, I knew I had to care for my child, no matter my mental state. As a Noncommissioned Officer (NCO) in the United States Air Force, I still had a duty to lead and care for my Airmen. I kept going, showing up every day, even when I felt completely broken inside. Days blurred into months, and before I realized it, two years had passed. I had been functioning, crying in the shadows, and doing just enough to fulfill my obligations because being strong felt like the only option I had.

When I got the news of my husband's passing, I was shattered. My soul felt lost. This wasn't how life was supposed to go. I questioned God, confused and heartbroken, trying to make sense of it all. Looking at my daughter was both painful and powerful. I didn't want to live but seeing her gave me strength. She saved my life.

Even though I was battling postpartum depression at the time, her presence gave me just enough light to keep going.

During that season, I didn't feel like myself. My identity as a wife, mother, and NCO felt disjointed. I didn't recognize the woman in the mirror. I had made all the right choices, married in love, built a family, pursued goals, and still, everything fell apart. I no longer saw myself as a priority. I simply functioned as a provider. It felt like I was living someone else's life, not the one I had planned.

Being strong meant showing up on days when I didn't want to get out of bed, putting on a smile when my heart was screaming. I would shut my office door under the guise of pumping, just to sit on the floor and cry. Then I'd wipe my face, gather myself, and walk out to lead my team like nothing was wrong. The strength people saw was just a mask, one I wore well, but one that was suffocating me behind the scenes.

Eventually, I reached a quiet breaking point. There was no dramatic moment, just a slow realization that I couldn't stay in survival mode forever. I was alive, but I wasn't really living. I didn't feel confident in my body, my energy was low, and my motivation had faded. Therapy helped me start to unpack all that I had been suppressing. I learned that healing was not weakness, it was necessary, and it was sacred.

My healing journey began with small but intentional acts of self-care. I focused on my health and appearance. I started going to the gym and making healthier meals. That one change became the spark. When my friends and family saw the shift in me, they rallied behind me. Their support helped pull me out of the isolation I had grown used to.

Today, I understand that grief and healing can coexist. I now know that being a good mother doesn't mean pretending everything is okay, it means showing up, even in the hard moments, and choosing to grow through them. If I could speak to the woman I was back then, I'd say, "Get up, Jennifer. You have to keep going. You *will* find happiness again."

- Jennifer Witherspoon, wife, mother, daughter, friend, Technical Sergeant, United States Air Force

My testimony: Unhealed Trauma

There was a season in my life when I lived entirely in survival mode without even realizing it. I was carrying toxic relationships, neglecting basic self-care, and pushing through chronic pain that slowly pulled me into depression. My body was inflamed, my emotions were overwhelmed, and I didn't recognize the connection between the two. Even in that darkness, the truth of "The Lord is close to the brokenhearted and saves those who are crushed in spirit" (Psalm 34:18) became an anchor for me.

As the stress increased, panic attacks began showing up without warning. I didn't understand at the time that they were connected to old, unhealed trauma from two car accidents I survived at ages 15 and 16. The fear and shock I had buried deep inside began resurfacing through anxiety and physical tension. It was frightening, but it reminded me of God's constant presence: "God is our refuge and strength, a very present help in trouble" (Psalm 46:1).

My healing began slowly, with small steps and a willingness to be honest with myself. I admitted that I wasn't okay and allowed myself to seek support physically, emotionally, and spiritually. I started caring for my body again, resting more intentionally, choosing healthier habits, and listening to what my pain was trying to tell me. Through it all, I kept returning to Jesus' invitation: "Come to me, all you who are weary and burdened, and I will give you rest" (Matthew 11:28).

Over time, survival mode loosened its grip on me. I released relationships that were draining, set healthy boundaries, faced my buried trauma, and allowed God to restore the places I had ignored for years. Healing came layer by layer, and I learned that God doesn't just pull us out of struggle, He walks with us through it, strengthening us along the way. Today I stand in a place of restoration, holding tightly to the promise that "He restores my soul" (Psalm 23:3).

-Moya Johnson, wife, mother, friend, Licensed Professional Counselor

My testimony: My Darkest Moment

There are things in life that you come to expect. You know one day that you will need to bury your parents, but a parent is not supposed to bury a child. I thought my darkest moment was when I went through my divorce. It turns out that my darkest moment was when someone decided to take my first-born son's life as if they gave it to him.

I still remember that day as if it were yesterday, and not nine years ago. I'd spoken to him asking him if him and his girlfriend wanted to come over for taco night. He told me no one wanted my salty tacos. That actually made me chuckle because for some reason they were on the salty side, and I couldn't figure out why. Well, I was seasoning the ground beef on top of adding the taco seasoning, but I digress. I laughed and said okay, I'll talk to you later.

Little did I know, that would be the last time I spoke to him. I received a call from my youngest son franticly telling me Robert had been shot, and I needed to get to the hospital. I called a couple of hospitals trying to find out which hospital I should proceed to, as there were several in the area. They told me where to go and to ask for security once I arrived.

I thought that maybe he'd been shot in the arm or something, and that we'd be leaving with him that evening. Instead, my reality was an officer showing me a photo of his body for me to identify. It looked as if he was lifeless. I will never forget the image of the tube in his mouth and lines of dry tears on his face.

Hours passed before a doctor came out and told me that he died from multiple gunshot wounds. My world as I knew it was crashing before me. I sat in disbelief and denial as shock set in and the painful reality that my beloved son was gone, and there was nothing I could do to bring him back to me.

Once I composed myself, I asked if I was able to see him? I needed to see my child that I'd once at the tender age of 16 given birth to in order to grasp the realization that he was really gone. I was told I was unable to see him in person because he was considered a crime scene. I begged and pleaded to see him. I told them that I would not touch him. I would look at him through a glass if needed. I just needed to see him in person so that my mind could process what I was being told was true. I was told no. I got home around midnight and cried the whole night.

I think I finally fell asleep around 4 or 5 am and woke up a few hours later hoping that it was all a horrible dream. As I sat dazed and confused trying to make sense of it all, I googled the incident and was able to find out from the news on their speculation of what may have happened.

Through this fog I recall thinking this was all a bad dream, and I needed to wake up from it. It wasn't a dream and my new reality and life as I knew it changed that dreadful night.

If you are not careful, this could be someone's darkest point of no return. I'm not sure how I'm still going, but God!

-Matilda Mahone, widow, mother, daughter, friend, Retired Chief Master Sergeant, United States Air Force

My testimony: Transformation and Purpose Found in Pain

There is a moment in every woman's life when she realizes she is starting over, and for me, that moment came the day I stood in the middle of my almost empty apartment. No noise, no comfort, no familiar routine, just silence, walls, and the question that echoed louder than anything else, *"Now what?"* That emptiness was more than physical; it was the darkness of feeling lost, alone, and unsure of what pieces of me would survive the shift my life had just taken. That kind of darkness is dangerous; it is a daily fight not to be pulled back into it.

Losing my marriage was painful, but losing my best friend, my brother of nearly thirty years, shattered me. His passing was sudden, unexpected, and it hit at a time when my life had already been turned upside down. Grief stacked on top of grief, and I could not imagine how I was supposed to keep going. That goodbye pierced me deeper than the divorce ever could.

Loneliness became my classroom; it taught me what community never could. It showed me that I could survive, that God was the only one I had left to lean on, and that in the stillness, I realized everything I lost was what He used to get my attention. But the hardest battles were the ones inside my own mind. The lies whispered to me that I was unloved; that I was unnecessary; that I was discarded; that no one would notice if I was no longer here. The identity I once held as a mother, the role that brought me the most joy, felt stripped from me, and that pain was unlike anything else.

Some days, I did not get out of bed. I cried until I could not. I starved without trying. I shrank into myself while attempting to make sense of everything. I went to a neurologist and was diagnosed with conversion disorder, which in my mind felt like another way of calling me "crazy." I did not feel understood; I felt broken.

Therapy saved my life! There was one session I will never forget, the day I accepted the truth that I needed to leave my marriage. It terrified me; but I finally understood that I could not heal in the same environment that wounded me. Acceptance came slowly, but it came, and it set me free. Therapy also made me redefine resilience. I once wore that word proudly, not realizing that it meant I had stayed in situations longer than I should have; suffering in silence; surviving instead of living. I was so focused on how my decisions would affect others that I did not consider how staying was damaging me.

The first boundary I set was saying "no." That simple word scared me; yet it protected me. I had spent my life putting others first, even when I had nothing left to give. For once, I had to face my own pain and choose myself. Loving people who did not show up for me became another wound I carried quietly. I continued to show up for them, but resentment began to grow inside me. When I needed them most, I received "you will be fine" energy, like my pain was not important.

But Act 2, the woman I am becoming now, is someone the younger me would be proud of. I speak up for myself. I set boundaries that honor my peace. I allow myself to take up space without apologizing. I process my feelings instead of burying them. I give myself the room to heal. And yes, I embrace my alone time without fear.

Healing for me looks like therapy, silence, boundaries, and choosing not to transfer my pain to others. It looks like accepting love and help without guilt; allowing myself to know that I am worthy and deserving. It looks like understanding that refusing kindness blocks my blessings and someone else's too. Even though I am still healing, I am no longer in survival mode, not in the way I once was. God is restoring me piece by piece.

I use my story now to help others who are walking through darkness similar to what I survived. My pain was not wasted. If my journey can guide even one person through their storm, then I still have purpose.

I have always known I was meant to be a wife and a mother. Even now, with no prospects in sight, I still believe I will be a wife again. I pray for clarity; for direction; for strength; and I trust God with what is next.

Life did not end for me; it simply evolved. I chose to live, and in choosing life, I discovered a new version of myself, a wiser version, a stronger version, a woman who is unlearning what broke her and relearning what will build her.

This is only the beginning of my Act 2.

-LaShronda Rodgers, friend, sister, daughter, mother, CEO of ReLY Consulting

My testimony: Grace, Mercy, and Purpose

I was raised in the church. My dad was a deacon, and my mom was a Sunday school teacher. Growing up, I had strict parents, and our lives centered around three places: church, school, and home. I made good grades, participated in band and sports, and worked hard. But even though I did well, I never really fit in. People put me on a pedestal, calling me "goody two shoes" and a "nerd." Their words stung, and though I kept a smile on my face, it hurt my feelings deeply. Still, I kept pushing forward, and God kept guiding my steps. "For I know the plans I have for you, declares the Lord, plans to prosper you and not harm you, plans to give you hope and a future." Jeremiah 29:11

I graduated with honors and received multiple academic, band, and sports scholarships. I thought I had my life planned out. But the summer before college, while attending a pre-college preparation program, I became pregnant. I was afraid to tell anyone; my parents, my friends, even the father. I didn't know how to handle it. My parents had always taught me to go to school, go to college, get married, and then build a family. I felt like I had messed up the "right order," and I was terrified, ashamed, and convinced my life was over.

I went on to college, went to band practices, performed at football games, and continued playing softball on scholarship. I practiced, slid across bases, lifted weights, and still never went to the doctor or took prenatal vitamins. I didn't even know I was pregnant at first, but soon I figured it out. I taped my stomach, wore big clothes, and tried my best to hide it. I lived in denial because I was afraid. I didn't want to disappoint my parents, embarrass my family, or become the topic of gossip.

But while I was trying to hide my situation from everyone else, I could never hide from God. "Behold, I am with you always, even unto the end of the world." Matthew 28:20

One weekend while visiting friends, I began bleeding and felt something was very wrong. Still, I didn't tell my parents. The pain grew stronger, it was what I now know were contractions. From 4 p.m. to about 9 p.m., I was in pain, alone in my room, scared and unsure of what to do. When I thought everyone was asleep, I ran a tub of water. I could have died that night. I wasn't thinking about life, safety, or consequences. All I felt was fear, shame, and hopelessness.

But God, He stepped in. "When you pass through the waters, I will be with you; and through the rivers, they shall not overflow you." Isaiah 43:2

God spoke to my mother at just the right moment. She came in and found me bleeding in the tub. I was crying, terrified. She helped me out and rushed me to the hospital. They ran tests and told her I was pregnant. I was immediately taken to labor and delivery. Everything was a blur, but one moment I remember clearly; they asked me if I wanted to keep my baby. Through tears, pain, and fear, I said yes.

I delivered my son on Easter morning, the same day we celebrate resurrection, new life, and redemption. On the day that symbolized new beginnings, God gave me mine. "His grace is sufficient for me, for His power is made perfect in weakness." 2 Corinthians 12:9

The look on my mother's face hurt more than childbirth itself. The shock, the disappointment, the hurt. And then came the judgment. Word traveled fast. Some people didn't show love, they celebrated my pain. I had to stand before the church and apologize for having a baby out of wedlock. The father denied him. And I thought my life was over. But God said, "Your life is just beginning." "For though the righteous fall seven times, they rise again." Proverbs 24:16

My son became my blessing. My parents supported me and helped me raise him. I continued my education. I didn't die in that bathroom. I didn't lose my mind. I didn't lose my son. I gained purpose. I gained strength. I gained a testimony. God made a way when I couldn't see a way. "And we know that all things work together for good to those who love God, to those who are called according to His purpose." Romans 8:28

Now, 27 years later, my son has grown into an amazing young man. God gave me what I needed when I didn't even know what I needed. He showed me that even when we fall short, His grace is greater. His love is deeper. His purpose is stronger.

My story is one of mistakes, mercy, and miracles. God spared my life. He gave me a blessing. And He turned my shame into purpose. "What the enemy meant for evil, God meant for good." Genesis 50:20

My testimony is simple: I could have died. I could have given up. I could have stayed in shame. But God stepped in. He saved me; physically, emotionally, and spiritually. God wasn't done with me then. And He's not done with me now.

-Alissa Wriley-Bafford, mother, daughter, grandmother, sister, wife, friend, educator

My testimony: Survival mode to Freedom

For years I lived in survival mode, the kind where you wake up already bracing for impact. I moved through life on autopilot, carrying burdens that were way too heavy for one person, but I did it anyway because I didn't feel like I had a choice. I learned how to smile when I was breaking, how to keep going when my tank was empty, and how to be strong for everyone except myself. People saw the strength, but they never saw the nights I cried myself to sleep or the silent battles I fought just to make it to the next day. Survival mode made me tough, but it also hardened me in ways I'm still untangling.

Then God stepped in and changed everything. He pulled me out of places I didn't even know I was trapped in. He slowed me down, softened me and showed me that I didn't have to fight every single thing by myself. All that pressure turned into purpose, all that fear shifted into faith, and the constant survival finally became peace. I didn't just make it out, I came out transformed. God reminded me that I wasn't designed to stay in survival mode forever.

I was designed to grow, to breathe, to rise, and to walk in the strength He placed in me long before the storm ever started.

-Natasha Huff Adams, mother, daughter, friend, author, Retired Master Sergeant, United States Air Force

As you've read the journeys of these seven women, I pray you felt something move within you; a tug, a whisper, a reminder that God is still in the business of transforming lives.

These testimonies were not placed here by accident. They are seeds. They are mirrors. They are proof. Proof that God meets us in the dark, walks us through the valley, and brings us out refined, restored, and renewed.

Each woman shared her story so you would know you're not alone, and more importantly, so you would know there is hope. If God did it for them, He can do it for you. Their deliverance is not a distant miracle, it's an invitation.

An invitation to believe again. To trust again. To rise again. To surrender again. To become again. My prayer is that as you close this chapter, you open a new one in your own life; one where healing is possible, forgiveness is attainable, peace is accessible, and transformation is inevitable.

Whatever you are walking through, God sees you. Whatever you survived, God already prepared purpose for it. Whatever you lost, God can restore. And whoever you are becoming, God is shaping with intentional grace.

May these pages remind you that brokenness is not the end, it is simply the place where God begins His greatest work. You are next. Your testimony is loading. And when your moment comes, when God shifts your story, may you have the courage to share it, just like these seven brave women did.

With love, grace, and unwavering belief in your becoming.

-Melissa Richey-Bridges, Empowerment Advocate

Embracing the Encounter

Recognizing God's presence during our trials doesn't necessarily change our circumstances immediately but transforms our perspective:

- Renewed Strength: An inner fortitude emerges, enabling us to face challenges with a renewed spirit.
- Deepened Faith: Experiencing God's closeness fosters a more intimate and trusting relationship.
- Purposeful Living: Understanding that our struggles have meaning can redirect our path toward healing and helping others.

Reflection:

Think back to a challenging period in your life. Can you identify moments where you sensed a divine presence or felt an inexplicable peace? Recognizing these encounters can strengthen your faith and provide comfort in future trials.

Chapter 4:
Caught and Carried:
Learning to Trust Divine Strength When Yours Is Gone

There comes a moment in every journey when our own strength waivers, and we find ourselves teetering on the edge of despair. In these vulnerable times, many discover an unwavering support that lifts them beyond their own capabilities. This chapter explores the transformative experience of relying on divine strength when our own is depleted, leading to personal renewal and the ability to uplift others without draining ourselves.

Recognizing Our Limitations

Life's challenges often push us to our limits, revealing the finite nature of our strength and resilience. It's in these moments of weakness that we confront our human fragility and the overwhelming weight of our burdens. Acknowledging our limitations is not a sign of defeat but a gateway to discovering a strength beyond our own.

The Divine Embrace

Just as a child instinctively reaches for a parent in times of fear or uncertainty, we too can turn to a higher power for comfort and strength. This divine embrace offers more than just solace; it provides a profound empowerment that enables us to navigate life's storms with renewed vigor. In these sacred moments, we realize that we are not alone, and that our struggles are being transformed into sources of strength.

Empowering Others Without Depletion

One of the most profound realizations in this journey is the ability to pour into others without draining oneself. By tapping into divine strength, we find an inexhaustible source of love and energy that allows us to uplift those around us. This balance ensures that our efforts to help others do not come at the expense of our own well-being.

Practical Steps to Embrace Divine Strength

1. Cultivate Daily Spiritual Practices: Engage in regular prayer, meditation, or reflection to connect with the divine source of strength.
2. Seek Supportive Communities: Surround yourself with individuals who uplift and encourage, creating a network of mutual support.
3. Serve Others Generously: Actively look for opportunities to help those in need, allowing the act of giving to replenish your own spirit.
4. Set Healthy Boundaries: Recognize your limits and ensure that your efforts to help others do not lead to personal burnout.

Reflection:

Consider a time when you felt your strength was insufficient to face a challenge. How did you find support, and what strengths did you discover within yourself during that period?

Chapter 5:
Healing from the Inside Out. The Beginning of Restoration: *Mind, Body, and Soul*

There's a moment after the breakdown, after the falling and the carrying, when you begin to feel the shift. It's subtle at first. A sigh. A deeper breath. A softer heart. A flicker of hope. That's when healing begins, not from the outside in, but from the **inside out.**

Healing is an inside job.

People may see your smile, your strength, your confidence. But only you, and God, know what it took to get there. True healing doesn't start with fixing the things around you. It starts with facing what's within you. The brokenness. The bitterness. The burdens. And choosing, sometimes moment by moment, to give those pieces to God and allow Him to do the mending.

Restoring the Mind

Your thoughts shape your reality. If pain and trauma rewired how you see yourself and the world, healing must begin by renewing your mind.

- Romans 12:2 says, "Be transformed by the renewing of your mind." That's where the restoration starts: in your thoughts, in your beliefs, in the way you speak to yourself.
- Healing the mind means unlearning the lies and relearning the truth: that you are worthy, chosen, loved, enough.
- It's giving yourself permission to rest, to feel, to grow. To stop rehearsing the pain and start rehearsing the promise.

Restoring the Body

Pain takes a toll on the body, even when it's emotional or spiritual. Healing from the inside out also means honoring your body as the vessel God gave you.
• For me, it looked like slowing down. Drinking water. Stretching. Moving. Resting. Eating to nourish, not punish.
• It also looked like paying attention to what my body was saying: where I felt tension, where I stored trauma, where I needed to release.

Your healing journey is sacred, and your body is part of that journey. God doesn't just want your heart whole. He wants your whole body being whole.

Restoring the Soul

The soul is the seat of your emotions, your will, your deepest truths. When life breaks you, it fractures the soul. Healing is where the real restoration happens.
• It happens in the stillness. In the surrender. In the conversations with God that nobody hears but Him.
• It happens when you forgive. When you let go. When you believe that joy is still possible, even after everything.

Your soul is where God does His most intimate work. He doesn't just heal it, He restores it. He revives it. He breathes new life into places that were lifeless.

From Surviving to Thriving

Healing isn't linear, and it isn't always pretty. But it is possible. And it's powerful. Because once you start healing from the inside out, the outside can't help but reflect what's happening within. You'll walk differently.

Speak differently. Love differently. Show up differently. Not because life got easier, but because you got stronger, whole and restored.

Reflection Questions:

• What areas of your life need inner healing? Your thoughts, your emotions, your body?
• What lies have you believed about yourself that need to be replaced with truth?
• How can you give yourself grace while you're still becoming?

Chapter 6:

The Lies We Believed: *Confronting the Inner Dialogue and Rewriting Your Truth*

Before you can walk fully in your purpose, you have to face the voice inside that's been holding you hostage. That voice that told you you're not good enough, not smart enough, not worthy of love, not qualified, not chosen. That voice didn't come from God, it came from pain.

The inner dialogue becomes the inner dictator.

Sometimes the worst things ever said to us weren't from other people, they were from **OURSELVES!** And sadly, those words didn't start with us. They came from seeds planted by rejection, abuse, disappointment, comparison, fear, and shame.

Over time, those seeds grew into weeds that choked our identity and distorted how we see ourselves. But healing means becoming aware. Confronting those lies. Challenging that inner critic. And choosing, on purpose, to rewrite the narrative with truth, love, and power. This is exactly why I wrote this book.

Step 1: Confronting the Dialogue

Ask yourself:
- What do I believe about myself?
- Who told me that?

• Is that belief rooted in truth or trauma?

You can't conquer what you won't confront. You have to call the lie out by name. Was it the lie that said you were too damaged? Too late? Too much? Too broken? Bring it into the light, because truth only sets you free when it's exposed.

Step 2: Rewriting the Narrative with Words of Affirmation

Affirmations are more than cute quotes or trendy captions. They are declarations. Weapons. Reminders of who God says you are, even when you don't feel like it.

Try these:
• I am worthy of healing.
• I am enough, just as I am.
• I release the lies I believed and embrace God's truth about me.
• I am no longer defined by my past.
• I am strong. I am chosen. I am becoming.

Speak life over yourself, especially on the days when it feels hardest to believe.

Step 3: Manifestation Through Alignment

Manifestation is not about wishing, it's about aligning. Aligning your words, your actions, your faith, and your energy with what you desire and believe is already yours in God's timing.

• When you affirm it, believe it.
• When you believe it, walk like it.

• When you walk like it, doors start opening that you didn't even knock on.
Manifesting healing means visualizing your wholeness and becoming the version of you who's already walking in freedom. Show up like him or her, **NOW!**

Step 4: Execution by Doing the Work

You can affirm it and manifest it, but if you don't do the work, you'll stay stuck. Healing takes action.

• That means setting boundaries.
• That means journaling, praying, going to therapy, changing environments.
• That means making decisions that match where you're going, not where you've been.

Execution is faith in motion. It's telling your future self, "I love you too much to stay here."

Your Truth:

God says:
• You are fearfully and wonderfully made (Psalm 139:14).
• You are more than a conqueror (Romans 8:37).
• You are chosen, royal, and set apart (1 Peter 2:9).
• You are not your mistakes. You are His masterpiece (Ephesians 2:10).

Let that be the truth that silences every lie.

Reflection Questions:

- What lie have you believed the longest?
- What truth do you need to start declaring today?
- What action can you take this week that aligns with your healing?

Chapter 7:

Made Whole, Not Perfect: *Embracing Imperfection While Healing*

Healing doesn't make you flawless. It makes you whole and there's a difference.

Wholeness is about integration, not perfection. It's about reclaiming the parts of you that were fractured and learning to live with your scars, not ashamed of them, but aware of what they taught you. It's about accepting that you can be a work in progress and still be worthy of love, peace, and joy.

Perfection is a myth. Grace is the truth.

Let's be clear, no one is perfect but God. Not the people you compare yourself to. Not the influencers with the filtered lives. Not the family members who pretend everything is okay. Everyone is healing from something. Everyone is learning. Everyone has something they've had to forgive, release, or outgrow. So why are we so hard on ourselves?

We say things like:

- "I should be further along."
- "I shouldn't feel this way anymore."
- "I messed up again. I must not be healing right."

But healing isn't a straight line. And falling short doesn't mean you failed. It means you're human. And you are not disqualified by your humanity. Healing isn't about never falling; it's about knowing who to fall into. When you mess up, grace is still available. When you regress, God still sees you. When the old thoughts try to come back, the new truth still stands.

You were never meant to heal by being perfect. You were meant to heal by being honest.
Give yourself grace.

Grace says:
• "It's okay to rest."
• "It's okay to not have it all together."
• "You're allowed to be proud of how far you've come, even if you're not where you want to be yet."

You're not broken because you still cry. You're not weak because you still feel the weight. You're not behind because you still need time. You are healing, and healing is holy.

Wholeness Looks Like:
• Waking up and choosing peace even when the past tries to haunt you.
• Forgiving yourself for not knowing what you didn't know.
• Showing up for your life, even if it's with shaky hands and tear-filled eyes.
• Celebrating small wins like they're big victories. (Because they are.)

Wholeness is when you stop chasing perfection and start embracing process.

What If God Is Proud of You, **Already?**

What if the grace you've been begging for is already wrapped around you? What if God isn't waiting for the "healed version" of you to show up, but instead, He's loving you right now, in this moment, in your mess? What if being whole simply means you've chosen to keep going, to believe again, to breathe deeper, and to forgive yourself and others? That's power. That's wholeness. That's healing.

Reflection Questions:

- Have you been placing pressure on yourself to be perfect in your healing?
- Where can you show yourself more grace?
- What does wholeness look like for you right now?

Chapter 8:

Purpose in the Pain: *Seeing How Your Wounds Can Become Your Witness*

Some of the most powerful things God will do in your life will start in the place that hurt you the most. That pain you tried to hide? That story you thought disqualified you? That moment you thought would break you? It didn't break you, it built you. And now you're standing on the other side, not perfect, but whole and with purpose.

There Was Always Purpose in It

Pain doesn't feel purposeful in the moment. It feels lonely, confusing, exhausting. But God wastes nothing. Not one tear. Not one heartbreak. Not one loss. Every ounce of it is being used to shape your calling, deepen your compassion, strengthen your voice, and give weight to your witness. The very thing you once cried about will become the thing that connects you to someone else's healing. You don't go through it just for you. You go through it so you can reach back and say, "I've been there, and here's how I made it through."

Your Pain Has a Platform, But Your Discernment Holds the Mic

Not everyone deserves access to your pain. Yes, your story matters. Yes, your healing journey is powerful. But every testimony doesn't need a public stage. Sometimes your healing was meant to water a select few. And that's okay. This is where discernment comes in.

God will show you who needs to hear your story. He'll tell you when to speak and how to share it. He'll protect your vulnerability by placing it in the right spaces. Discernment keeps your pearls from being thrown to swine. There will be people who only want your story for gossip, not growth. Others will try to reduce your pain to drama, instead of recognizing it as deliverance. That's why you have to stay in tune with the Holy Spirit. He'll lead you in truth, timing, and trust.

You're Not Just a Survivor, You're a Vessel

You didn't just survive. You transformed and evolved. And now, you're a safe space. You're a lighthouse. You're a voice for someone who hasn't found theirs yet. Your wounds are no longer open. They've been turned into wisdom. And your scars? They're not shameful, they're sacred. Proof of what God brought you through.

Don't Be Afraid to Testify

You're not being "too much" by sharing your truth. You're being a mirror for someone who doesn't know healing is possible. The pain you've endured has given your voice authority. When you speak chains can break, hope can rise, and darkness can lift. That's what it means to have purpose in your pain.

Reflection Questions:

• What painful part of your story do you feel called to share?
• Who do you feel safe and led to share it with?
• How can your story become a testimony for someone else?

Chapter 9:

Rising from the Ashes: *Becoming New, Stepping Into Your Next Season*

There's a moment in every healing journey when you look back and realize: I made it. Not because life got easier. Not because the pain magically disappeared. But because you chose to keep going when everything in you wanted to give up. You survived what was sent to break you. And now, **YOU RISE!** .

I Am the Courage That Rose from the Struggles

I've been tested.
I've been challenged.
I've walked through storms that tried to silence me, strip me, and stop me. But here I stand, stronger, wiser, and unstoppable.

I am not defined by what I went through.
I am defined by how I rose from it.

Every struggle, every setback, every tear only built the courage inside me.
I am the proof that pain has purpose. That trials shape strength. That resilience is born in the fire.

So when you see me standing tall, know this:
I didn't break. I built.
I didn't quit. I conquered.
And I will keep rising.

My 45th Birthday Solo Trip: The Year of Freedom

Phuket.
Kuala Lumpur.
Bali.

Each stop on that solo trip was more than a destination, it was a declaration. It was power. It was transformative. It was my mirror of truth.

I stepped into a new chapter, one of freedom, joy, and limitless possibilities. It wasn't just a vacation, it was a rebirth.

This is my year of freedom:
Free to dream.
Free to grow.
Free to love.
Free to be unapologetically ME.

No more limits.
No more waiting.
Just walking boldly in purpose and power.

That trip taught me that healing is real. That starting over is possible. And that God will often take you across the world to remind you of who you are.

Becoming New

To rise from the ashes means something had to be burned down. Old beliefs. Old fears. Old versions of yourself. And that's okay. Because God isn't trying to rebuild the old you.

He's creating something new; something stronger, deeper, and more aligned with your purpose.

This is your resurrection season. You're not who you were. You're who you've become: graced, grounded, and glowing in God's love. If There's One Thing Life Has Taught Me, it's this: You are never too old, never too late, and never too bound to break free and become who you were meant to be.

And if you're reading this wondering if you've missed your moment, let me remind you:
Your moment is now. Your rise is happening. And your next season starts the moment you believe again.

Reflection Questions:

• What ashes have you risen from?
• What "old" version of yourself are you ready to release?
• What does your new season look like?

Affirmation:

I am not my past. I am my progress. I rise boldly into my next season, knowing I carry wisdom, grace, and unshakable purpose. I am becoming all God created me to be; freely, fully, and fearlessly.

Chapter 10:

Living Authentically Free: *Walking Daily in Purpose, Healing, and Divine Love*

There's nothing more powerful than a healed woman walking in her purpose. Not perfect.

Not untouched by pain. But free authentically, boldly, and unapologetically. When you've been through the fire, cried yourself to sleep, questioned your worth, and still found the strength to get up again, that's when freedom becomes a lifestyle.

Authenticity Is the Real Glow-Up

Living authentically free means no longer shrinking to make others comfortable. No longer masking your pain or pretending you're okay just to keep the peace. It means standing tall in your truth, even when your voice shakes. It means allowing God to lead, not fear. Peace, not performance. Purpose, not perfection. You are allowed to be all of who you are: flawed, healing, gifted, and still growing. That is what makes you powerful. That is what makes you free.

Purpose: The Fruit of My Freedom

One of the most beautiful outcomes of healing is clarity, and from that clarity comes purpose. This is why I created Empower and Evolve Solutions Consulting. I didn't just want to heal for myself. I wanted to be a vessel for others, especially teen girls and women who've been overlooked, overwhelmed, or silenced. Through mentoring and coaching, I get to help others tap into their voice, their value, and their vision.

It's more than a business, it's a calling. It's a movement. It's ministry through mindset. It's coaching with compassion. It's leadership birthed from life experiences. Every time I pour into someone else's growth, I'm reminded of what God brought me through, and that nothing I endured was in vain. Empower and Evolve is my "yes" to purpose. It's where my healing meets my mission. It's how I live authentically free and authentically ME.

Divine Love: My Daily Anchor

I no longer chase validation, because I've already been chosen. I don't have to perform for love, because I'm loved by the Creator of love itself. Living in divine love means I walk with assurance, not anxiety. With gratitude, not guilt. With power, not people pleasing. God's love is my safe place. It's where I found my identity, my peace, and my wholeness. And it's what I wake up in every day. This love isn't based on what I do, it's based on who He is. And because of that, I am free to grow, evolve, lead, and love without fear.

This Is the Becoming

You don't have to wait for perfect conditions to start walking in freedom. You just have to decide: No more pretending. No more hiding. No more shrinking. This is your season to show up as you: healed, whole, and walking in divine alignment. The life you desire isn't something you have to chase. It's something you create by showing up in truth, loving yourself fully, and letting God lead.

Reflection Questions:

- What does living authentically free mean to you?
- In what ways are you being called to help others?
- How can you align your daily actions with your divine purpose?

Declaration:

I am walking boldly in my purpose. I am free to be all God called me to be. I am aligned, healed, and empowered. My life is a reflection of divine love, daily growth, and unshakable freedom. I no longer just survive. I lead, I evolve, and I live authentically free.

Chapter 11:

The Sacred Pause: *When God Sits You Down to Raise You Up*

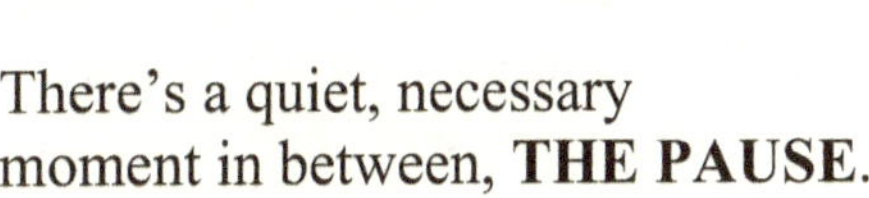

There's a quiet, necessary moment in between, **THE PAUSE**.
The waiting room.
The hidden season where God sits you down to refine, teach, prune, and reposition.

It doesn't come with applause.
It doesn't look glamorous.
It doesn't feel exciting.
It doesn't feel like promotion.
But it's holy ground.

In fact, it often looks like rejection, feels like stillness, and whispers like silence.

But this pause isn't punishment.
It's preparation.

It's where God does His deepest work, not on stages, but in the stillness.

This is where wounds become wisdom, gifts become grounded, and identity becomes rooted. It's the season where everything external slows down so what's internal can finally grow up.

It's where platforms are stripped, performances end, and masks fall away, leaving only the real you in the presence of a real God.

For me, the pause came after 23 years of nonstop military service. I had spent over two decades in the military, serving, leading, surviving. And when I retired, I thought I'd immediately pivot into purpose with clarity and momentum. But God had other plans. He didn't just release me from a job, He invited me into stillness. And it was in that stillness that I met the version of myself I had been too busy to hear.

When God Sits You Down

My sacred pause began when I transitioned from military life to civilian life. The uniform came off, the duties were over, and for the first time in a long time, I had space to breathe. The noise of leadership, responsibility, and constant motion went silent. And in that silence, I found myself face-to-face with myself. No more ranks. No more deployments. Just me, my thoughts, and a God who refused to let me stay surface level.

I was still healing. Still rediscovering who I was outside the uniform. Still learning to say "yes" and "no" from a place of authenticity, not obligation. That in itself was divine. I had been so used to pouring out, I didn't even know what it felt like to pour in.

When the Platform Is Pulled

When God removes your platform, He's not punishing you, He's protecting what He plans to build. For me, the biggest platform He took wasn't a stage, it was a marriage. That divorce stripped me to the core. I didn't just lose a relationship; I lost the version of myself that had been performing to survive. I had to rebuild my self-worth, brick by brick, in front of two little legacies (my children) who were watching me rise.

When God took away my marriage, I discovered a deeper love and respect for myself that I didn't even know existed. I had been belittled for so long, I started to believe it. But the pause exposed the lies and made room for truth. I wasn't just rebuilding my life, I was rebuilding my foundation.

Rest as Warfare

I didn't know what rest truly was until I retired. I had been in motion for so long, I thought rest was laziness. I thought slowing down meant falling behind. But God began to show me that rest is not weakness, it's warfare. In rest, I found freedom. In stillness, I found strategy. In solitude, I found peace. And most of all I found Him. He began to show me things I would've missed if I stayed busy, especially the one thing I had been praying for: patience. That rest taught me that delay isn't denial; it's divine alignment.

Obedience in Obscurity

Let me be honest and very clear, I didn't always obey in the dark. There were times I chose convenience over calling. I knew what God was saying, but I still did it my way. Obedience didn't come all at once. It was slow and then suddenly, I realized I had surrendered. I didn't get a certificate or a spotlight. What I got was internal transformation. He began to shift how I spoke, how I thought, how I carried myself. And in the darkness, I built something that would support my light: self-confidence. Funny thing? Everyone thought I had it all along. But confidence isn't performance, it's peace. And mine was finally real.

Being Benched or Being Built?

The pause didn't feel like punishment, it felt like a divine time-out. A space to reflect on what I allowed, what I tolerated, and what I was created for. I wasn't forgotten. I was being forged. I realized this fully during a powerful event I hosted called "The Transformation Experience". Sixteen women. One room. Honest stories. Bold breakthroughs. And in that moment, I saw it. This wasn't just something I created. It was the fruit of everything God had built in the dark. The pause produced power. I walked into that room no longer questioning my voice, my worth, or my assignment. I had been hidden, now I was ready.

Spiritual Anchors

One scripture carried me through when the silence felt too loud: Psalm 5:3, "In the morning, Lord, you hear my voice; in the morning I lay my requests before you and wait expectantly." That one verse reminded me that God hears me, even in the pause. And while I wait, He's definitely working.

Prepared in the Pause

Looking back now, I realize: there are parts of my becoming that could only be birthed in the pause. Being mentally free. Reclaiming my voice. Walking in purpose without performance. I couldn't have done that on the platform, I had to be processed privately. The sacred pause wasn't about delay. It was about depth.

Reflection Questions

1. Are you in a "pause" season right now? What might God be trying to teach you?
2. What platform has been removed in your life, and what new foundation is being laid?
3. Where are you being called to rest, obey, or release?
4. Can you see how being benched was actually preparation?

A Prayer for the Hidden Season

God, thank You for sitting me down. Even when I didn't understand it, even when I resisted it, You knew what I needed. Thank You for the quiet spaces where You spoke louder than the world. Thank You for rest that renews, obedience that refines, and love that doesn't require performance. Teach me to trust the pause. Strengthen me in the silence. And help me rise with power when the time comes. I trust You, even here. Amen.

Chapter 12:

Gratitude in the Growing:
Finding Joy Even in Progress

It's easy to speak about gratitude when everything is going right. When the doors open, the blessings pour in, and life feels good, our gratitude flows freely. But what about the in-between moments? What about when we're still healing, still waiting, still unsure of how it will all come together? That's where real gratitude is born, not from perfection, but from perspective.

When Growth Feels Like a Grind

There are seasons where it feels like nothing is working in your favor. You pray and still cry. You give and still feel empty. You hope and still wrestle with fear. And in those moments, it's tempting to complain, to compare, to question:

"Why is this happening?"
"When will it be my turn?"
"Why does it feel like I'm being overlooked?"

But here's the truth: growth often feels like resistance before it reveals progress. It's messy. It's uncomfortable. But it's necessary.

Mindset Shift: From Frustration to Fulfillment

Choosing gratitude in the middle of growth requires a mindset shift. It's not about denying what you're going through, it's about deciding how you'll respond to it.

Instead of saying:

• "Nothing is working," say "Something is shifting, even if I can't see it yet."
• "I'm stuck," say "I'm being still so I can hear what God is saying."
• "I'm tired of waiting," say "I'm being prepared for something greater."

Speak life. Speak truth. Speak what you want to see, not just what you feel in the moment. Your words have power, and your thoughts shape your experience. Gratitude isn't a feeling, it's a decision.

Joy in the Small Things

Gratitude teaches us to find beauty in the little moments:

• A peaceful morning.
• A deep breath.
• A kind word.
• A lesson learned.
• A door that didn't open; because it wasn't meant to.

When you start to celebrate the "small" blessings, you begin to see just how rich your life truly is. Joy isn't reserved for milestones. It lives in moments; tiny, sacred, everyday moments that remind you: I'm still here. I'm still growing. And that is enough.

Gratitude Grows You

Gratitude isn't just about saying "thank you." It's about seeing your journey through the lens of faith. It's realizing that even in pain, there's purpose. Even in delays, there's development. Even in the waiting, there's wonder.

When you start practicing gratitude intentionally, everything shifts. You feel lighter. You move with more grace. You trust deeper. You love harder. Because gratitude opens your heart to receive what God is doing, even when you don't fully understand it yet.

Reflection Questions:

• Where in your life can you practice more gratitude?
• What small moments have brought you joy recently?
• How can you reframe your current season through a lens of faith?

Affirmation:

I am grateful for who I am and who I am becoming. I speak life, I choose joy, and I trust the process. Even in the growing, I find peace. Even in the waiting, I worship. Gratitude is my posture, and joy is my portion.

Chapter 13:

No More Running. The Final Shift:

From Survival to Surrender

Some people walk around in survival mode their entire lives. Not because they want to, but because it's all they've ever known. They've learned to smile through heartbreak. To hold it all together, even while breaking silently inside. To stay busy, stay strong, stay distracted because slowing down would mean feeling everything they've been running from. But, you weren't created just to survive. You were made to live. To breathe. To heal. To love. To rest in God's presence without performing, pretending, or pushing past your pain.

Survival Mode

There's a version of me that existed in survival mode for far too long. She smiled when she wanted to scream. She showed up for everyone **EXCEPT** herself. She made being "strong" look easy, but inside she was unraveling. Survival mode isn't living. It's existing. It's functioning with a numb heart and an exhausted soul. It's waking up each day wondering if you'll make it to the next and pretending like you're fine in between. It's pouring out of an empty cup, keeping it together on the outside while falling apart on the inside.

I didn't even know I was in survival mode until I got still. Stillness exposed everything I'd buried under busyness, responsibility, and pain. And it terrified me. But that stillness was the beginning of my healing. I had to admit: I was tired of performing. Tired of pretending. Tired of surviving when I was created to thrive.

It started small, just breathing and being. Talking to God without a filter. Letting the tears fall and not apologizing for the broken places. I gave myself permission to feel. To rest. To receive. To believe that maybe, just maybe, God wasn't done with me.

I surrounded myself with truth. With people who saw the real me and didn't flinch. With scriptures that reminded me I was never alone. With grace for every day I didn't feel strong or whole. And slowly, I came back to life. Not all at once. But breath by breath. Prayer by prayer. Tear by tear.

I didn't just get through survival mode. I evolved through it. And now? I live. I feel. I hope. I trust. I thrive. Because God doesn't just rescue us from the fire, He rebuilds us in the ashes.

The Shift

There comes a moment when the run turns into a release. That moment where something in you says:
"I want healing more than I want hiding."
"I'm done pretending I'm okay."
"I can't carry this alone anymore."

And in that sacred moment when you stop fighting to look strong, That's where God meets you. Not at the finish line. Not when it all makes sense. But right in the middle of your mess. He doesn't flinch at your flaws. He doesn't retreat from your wreckage. He leans in with love that restores, revives, and rebuilds.

From Survival to Surrender

For so long, survival was your default setting.
• You did what you had to do.
• You held it down for everyone else.
• You tucked away your tears, your needs, your dreams just to make it through another day.

But survival is not the same as living. And God didn't call you to just get by, He called you to be whole. Surrender isn't weakness, it's wisdom. It's saying, "I no longer have to do this alone." It's releasing control and picking up peace. It's laying down pain and stepping into purpose

The Inside Out Healing

This whole journey, every chapter, every revelation has been about this: Healing from the inside out. Letting go of the guilt you carried. Rewriting the lies you believed. Loving the parts of you that used to feel unworthy. Walking in joy, even while you're still becoming. This is no longer about pretending. This is about presence: being here, being real, and being whole.

No More Running

You've run long enough.
From pain.
From truth.
From yourself.

But now, you return.

To yourself.

To God.
To peace.
To purpose.

You are no longer that broken woman or man who had to keep pushing just to be okay.

You are her/him, the one who was becoming the whole time.
Even when she/he didn't feel ready.
Even when she/he didn't feel seen.
Even when she/he didn't feel strong.

This is your moment.

- To be free.
- To be whole.
- To surrender without fear.
- To stop surviving and start living in grace.

You don't have to run anymore.

Let God carry you.

How I knew When I Needed to Stop Running

Somewhere between the past and the promise, I heard God whisper, "You're ready." And if you listen close, you'll hear the whisper that changed everything.

Reflection Questions:

• What survival patterns have you been holding onto?
• What would surrender look like in this season of your life?
• Are you ready to stop running and start becoming?

Final Declaration:

I release the need to survive. I surrender to healing, to wholeness, and to God's divine plan for my life. I no longer run from pain I run toward purpose. I trust that I am becoming the woman or man I was always meant to be. Fully, freely, and fearlessly.

Chapter 14:

Becoming Journal: *Reflections*

Introducing Your Becoming Journal

This isn't just a book you read, it's a journey you walk. And every step you take deserves reflection, intention, and grace. The **Becoming Journal** is your sacred space to pause, process, and participate in your own healing. These pages were created to help you go deeper, beyond the words, beyond the pain, and into the heart of your evolution.

Here, you can:

- Reflect on what's rising in you.
- Release what no longer serves you.
- Reaffirm the truth about who you are.
- Pray through the parts of you still healing.
- Take aligned action toward your freedom.

There's no right way to use these pages, just an honest way. Show up as you are: messy, growing, healing, becoming. This is your space. Your voice. Your becoming. Let's begin.

MY BECOMING JOURNAL

1. What's Stirring in Me?

What thoughts, emotions, or memories came up while reading this book?

2. What Am I Ready to Release?

Is there a belief, pattern, or fear that no longer serves who I'm becoming?

3. Affirming My Becoming

Write three statements that speak life over this part of your journey.

I am

____

I will

____

I trust

____

4. Prayer Prompt

Dear God, today I surrender…

5. Becoming in Action

What is one small action I can take this week that aligns with my healing?

____

____

____

____

____

____

____

____

____

____

____

____

Mini Declaration:

I am not who I was. I am becoming who I was created to be…on purpose, with power, and in divine peace.

Your Final Becoming Reflections

As you close this chapter of your healing journey, I invite you to write two sacred letters; ones that will help you honor your past, release your pain, and step boldly into who you are becoming. Take your time. Be honest. Be gentle with yourself. These letters are for your freedom.

1. A Letter to Your Younger Self

What does the little girl or boy inside of you need to hear? What truth do they deserve to know? What comfort, love, or affirmation would have changed everything?

Dear Younger Me…

2. A Letter to the Pain That Once Pursued You

Give your pain a voice and then take your power back. What would you say to the thing that chased you, shaped you, or silenced you? It's time to tell your pain the truth and release it.

Dear Pain…

I am no longer who I was.
I am who I've become.
Healed.
Whole.
Free.

Dear **You Who Are *Becoming*,**

If you've made it this far, let me say this, you are courageous. You didn't just read a book, you walked through a journey. A journey of facing your truth, releasing your pain, and beginning again.

Whether you're a woman rediscovering her worth, or a man reclaiming his identity, this book wasn't just about me. It was about you. About your story, your healing, your evolution. You may have stumbled through brokenness. You may have felt forgotten in the crowd. You may have cried silent tears in the dark, fighting battles no one ever saw. But still…You're here.
Still standing. Still becoming. Still rising.

And I want you to know something: You are not your pain. You are not your past. You are not what broke you. You are everything God says you are: chosen, loved, called, and created with purpose. There will still be moments when life feels heavy. Days when old wounds try to whisper lies. But now you've been equipped. You've been reminded. You've been empowered.

You don't have to run anymore. You can breathe. You can heal. You can show up fully, freely, and unapologetically. Because now you know: You were never too broken to be made whole. You were never too late to evolve. And you were never alone. God was always with you, carrying you even when you couldn't walk. So wherever life takes you from here, may you walk in freedom, live with boldness, and never again shrink to fit into places you've outgrown.

Thank you for letting me speak to your soul. Thank

you for trusting me with your heart. And thank you, for becoming.

With love, truth, and power,

Melissa Richey-Bridges

Acknowledgments

First and foremost, I give all honor and glory to God, the One who met me in my brokenness, carried me through the fire, and called me into purpose. Without Him, there would be no healing, no message, no becoming. Every page of this book is a reflection of His grace, mercy, and love.

To my children, you are my heartbeat. Thank you for being the reason I keep going, keep growing, and keep evolving. You've seen me rise, and I pray this journey reminds you that you, too, can rise from anything.

To my family, thank you for loving me through every season. Your prayers, your presence, and your support have held me up in ways I can't even put into words.

To my friends and tribe, the ones who saw the real me, who checked on me, cheered for me, cried with me, and never let me quit, you are divine assignments. Thank you for being safe spaces and sound voices during my process.

To my mentors and spiritual leaders, thank you for pouring wisdom, truth, and encouragement into me. Your impact helped shape the woman and the warrior I am today.

To every reader, supporter, and soul who picked up this book: **THANK YOU**. Thank you for trusting me with your time, your heart, and your healing. I don't take it lightly. My hope is that these words will meet you exactly where you are and gently guide you toward where you're meant to be.

To those who've ever felt broken, lost, overlooked, or forgotten, this book is for you. May it remind you that your pain has purpose, your voice has power, and your life is not over. It's just beginning.

And finally, to the version of me who almost gave up: Thank you for holding on. Look at us now, we didn't just survive. **WE BECAME!**

Founding Reader Recognition

Blessings family and thank you so much for your pre-order! I'm praying God covers you with favor, peace, and protection, and that this release pours strength, joy, and fresh hope into your life. You are appreciated.

- *Pankey Wallace*
- *Aleacha Philson*
- *Joie Macabasco*
- *Evelyn Tate*
- *Kimberly Lowe*
- *Hattie S. Petty*
- *Bobbie Richey*
- *Avis McCaslin*
- *Matilda Mahone*
- *Janice Presha*
- *Shakila Grate*
- *LaKisha Whitest*
- *Abigail Esparza*
- *Bruchell Washington*
- *Brandy Tate*
- *Nitiya Barry*
- *Nicole Shelton*
- *Teresa Doss*
- *Iesha Stanley*
- *Zakia Tate*
- *Shikeeta Barry*

Melissa Richey-Bridges

Melissa Richey-Bridges is a retired U.S. Air Force Chief Master Sergeant, mentor, speaker, and transformational author who has dedicated her life to helping women heal, grow, and evolve. After 23 years of military service, she stepped boldly into her next assignment of empowering others through faith filled leadership, emotional clarity, and authentic storytelling.

As the founder of *Empower & Evolve Solutions Consulting*, Melissa guides men and mostly women and teen girls through purpose-driven coaching, mindset work, and personal development. Her writing is rooted in transparency and grace, drawing from her own experiences of breaking, rebuilding, and becoming.

Melissa is known for her bold voice, heart-centered wisdom, and unwavering belief that every woman has the power to rise beyond her pain. Through her books, programs, and speaking, she is committed to helping others embrace healing, walk in purpose, and evolve from the inside out.

Scan the QR code below to connect with Melissa.

Zoë Life Publishing

Zoë Life Publishing is a publishing imprint that releases titles committed to offering encouragement and that are life transforming. We desire for our titles to impact readers in a way that is beyond entertainment; a way that will bring healing, restoration, or even productivity to one's life.

Scan the QR code below to visit our website today for more information.

www.ingramcontent.com/pod-product-compliance
Lightning Source LLC
LaVergne TN
LVHW090616110826
845146LV00001B/415

* 9 7 9 8 9 9 2 7 3 6 0 5 2 *